IMAGES OF ENGLAND

OLD GATESHEAD

The coat of arms of the old County Borough of Gateshead, prior to 1974. The goat's head reflected the general belief about the origin of the town's name (see p. 9). The motto has more than one interpretation, but it is generally taken to mean 'The head thrusts itself through the clouds'.

IMAGES OF ENGLAND

OLD GATESHEAD

ALAN BRAZENDALE

The author wearing Gateshead's mayoral robes and chain. The robes, hat, jabot and gloves have been the style worn on formal occasions since 1851. In that year, over 100 ladies, led by Mrs Hawkes, wife of the borough's first mayor, presented the borough with the chain and badge of office, which are still in use today.

First published 2000
Reprinted 2003, 2004, 2006

Reprinted in 2008 by
The History Press
The Mill, Brimscombe Port,
Stroud, Gloucestershire, GL5 2QG
www.thehistorypress.co.uk

Reprinted 2011, 2015

British Library Cataloguing in Publication Data.
A catalogue record for this book is available from the British Library.

ISBN 978 0 7524 2073 8

Typesetting and origination by
Tempus Publishing Limited.
Printed and bound in England.

Contents

Central Gateshead seen from Newcastle in an engraving from 1835.

Preface

It gives me great pleasure to write this preface to *Old Gateshead*. Alan Brazendale is a friend of many years' standing who is not only a well-known writer and lecturer on local history but is himself a former mayor of the borough. It is difficult to think of a more appropriate person to produce such a book about old Gateshead.

When we look at Gateshead today, we see a modern town surrounded by attractive open countryside and containing landmarks like the International Stadium, the Metro Centre and the Angel of the North, along with the Baltic Centre for Contemporary Art, the Gateshead Music Centre and the Millennium Bridge.

The Gateshead of the nineteenth and early twentieth centuries which is pictured in this book was very different. To begin with, it was much smaller, covering a fraction of the area and containing only half the population of the modern borough. Much of the filth and squalor left by the industrial revolution was still in evidence, especially in the riverside area, and although many advances were made during the nineteenth century, the massive programmes of slum clearance and rebuilding which have created modern Gateshead did not really begin until later in the twentieth century.

It has been said that it is only by understanding the past that we can really understand the present. I hope that this reminder of the 'old days', whether good or bad, will contribute to that understanding.

Pitch Wilson
Mayor of Gateshead (2002)

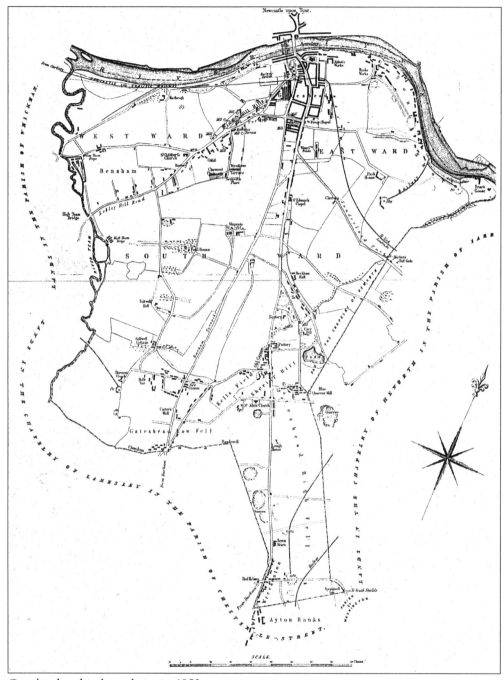

Gateshead and its boundaries in 1850.

Introduction

To say that this book is about 'Old Gateshead' is really using the word 'old' in two senses, because it not only contains photographs dating from the beginning of the twentieth century, but it is also concerned with 'old' Gateshead as it existed before its boundaries were extended in the 1930s and 1970s. The 1850 map on the opposite page shows the borough as it was prior to these changes.

A human settlement of some sort has almost certainly existed in Gateshead since at least Roman times. Indeed, although its name is usually accepted as being derived from 'Goats' Head', meaning a headland roamed by wild goats, an alternative explanation is that it means the 'head of the road (gate)', i.e. where the Roman road from the south ended at the river crossing. This latter suggestion reflects a growing awareness that the Roman presence in the Gateshead area was probably of much greater significance than was previously believed. This has been confirmed by recent excavations in the Bottle Bank area which have unearthed a number of important finds indicating the existence of a substantial Roman settlement.

An important Roman road junction probably also existed in southern Gateshead. The Wrekendyke branches off from the aforementioned road from the south at Wrekenton, where there may have been a Roman fort, and runs north-eastwards to *Arbeia*, the Roman supply base at South Shields. The discovery of the Whickham Washingwell fort by Professor Norman McCord in 1970 has led to speculation that the Stanegate, the Roman frontier line before the building of Hadrian's Wall, may have run through the south of Gateshead with the Wrekendyke as its eastern end. This theory is illustrated in the speculative map overleaf.

The first recorded mention of Gateshead, however, was not until Saxon times, when the Venerable Bede referred to an Abbot of Gateshead called Utta in AD 653. Gateshead later acquired some claim to fame as the site of the murder of the first Norman Bishop of Durham in 1080.

From Norman times, the Tyne was recognized as the boundary between the separate towns of Gateshead and Newcastle, but as Newcastle grew in economic importance, it made increasing efforts to control the affairs of its rival on the south bank of the river. In the early Middle Ages, these related to control of the bridge over the river, restrictions on the right to hold markets and the like, but in the sixteenth century, with the growth of coal-mining south of the river, Newcastle made vigorous attempts to annex Gateshead. These attempts were ultimately unsuccessful, but Newcastle did manage to acquire commercial control not only of the coal mines in the joint manors of Gateshead and Whickham (at that time the most important coalfield in the world), but also of all shipments from the Tyne, and of the Saltmeadows (riverside) area of Gateshead which later became a major centre of the iron and chemical industries.

It was only in the later nineteenth century and, increasingly, in the twentieth century, that Gateshead began to emerge from beneath the long shadow of Newcastle. The pictures in this book date from the early stages of that process.

Alan Brazendale
2000

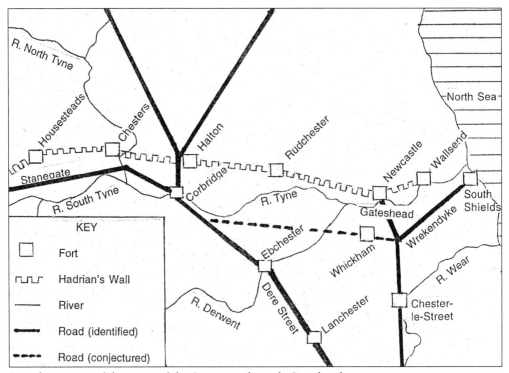

Speculative map of the route of the Stanegate through Gateshead.

One

Farming and Industry

Although it is difficult to visualize now, old Gateshead was predominantly an agricultural area until about the middle of the nineteenth century, much of it consisting of great estates which had been occupied by the local landed gentry since early medieval times. The development of coal-mining initially had little effect on farming. Much farming work was done by women and the seasonal nature of both farming and mining meant that men could work at one job or the other at different times of the year.

Later on, the transport of coal by waggonway and ship led to the growth of trades associated with engineering, rope-making and ship-building. Later still, for technological reasons, the chemical industry and glass-making became important. This increasing industrialization led to both industry and housing encroaching on the available land, and farming was progressively phased out, although some farms survived until the 1930s.

Initially, industrial development tended to be concentrated along the riverside, although other industries, often dating back to medieval times and in decline by the end of the nineteenth century, were more dispersed. These included, for example, quarrying, mainly for grindstones, pottery-making and clay pipe manufacture.

Shipcote West Farm, c. 1918. The Shipcote estate was the biggest estate in Gateshead and comprised two farms. The farmhouse was demolished in 1931 and the Leisure Centre was later built on the site.

Shipcote (later Dryden's) Farm, 1939. This was the other farm on the Shipcote estate which survived rather longer. It was built over during the 1920s and 1930s and the farm building itself was demolished during the Second World War. The fire station now stands on the site.

Derwent Crook Farm in 1936. Derwent Crook was a small estate to the west of Low Fell which was acquired by the Liddells of Ravensworth in the 1760s. The eastern part became building land in the early twentieth century and the western part was absorbed into Team Valley Trading Estate. This farm building was replaced by a garage.

Haymaking at Greenwell Farm in the 1930s. Lyndhurst (formerly Greenwell) School was later built on the site of the farmhouse.

Floods in Team Valley in 1886. The landscape is completely rural, with commercial and industrial development in the far distant future. (Compare the pictures on this page with those on p. 28.)

A view across Team Valley in 1934. This view is towards the west from Bensham. The scenery is still almost completely rural with only a few houses, mainly centred on Lobley Hill, at the top right. Construction of Team Valley Trading Estate started two years later.

The last mill on Bensham Bank, early in the twentieth century. Corn mills are a natural concomitant of farming and Gateshead seems to have been a major milling centre for County Durham with large numbers of mills, especially on the Windmill Hills, as the name implies. Most of the mills had ceased to function by the mid-nineteenth century and were later demolished.

The last mill in Gateshead. Snowdon's Mill at Blue Quarries stood as a ruin until it was demolished in 1964.

The Salte Well in Saltwell Road, rebuilt 1872. One of the major needs of a rural economy is a supply of clean water and Gateshead is still dotted with the sites of medieval wells. The Salte Well is notable in that it gave its name to one of Gateshead's great estates and subsequently to Gateshead's principal park.

Carter's Well, Durham Road, Low Fell, built *c.* 1836 (see also p. 71).

Sugar Well on Ravensworth Golf Course, c. 1933. The names of wells often related to the flavour of the water.

A surprising find in Bensham Road, 1937. This well was discovered during road works.

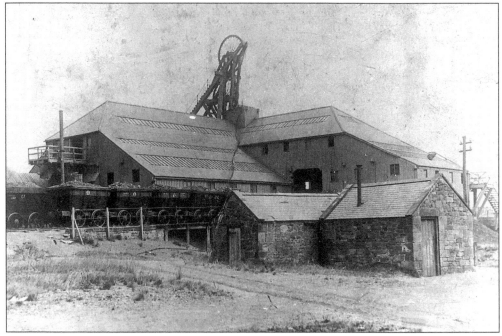

Team Colliery, Low Fell, early in the twentieth century. By the end of the nineteenth century most of the coal near to the river had been worked out and the collieries which remained tended to be in the southern part of the county borough area.

Management and workers at the Fanny Pit, Sheriff Hill, c. 1921. The pit closed in 1926. In accordance with local custom, the three interconnected shafts were named after the proprietors – John, Ada and Fanny (father, mother and daughter of the Southern family).

Ravensworth Ann Colliery, 1947. This is the first tub drawn after the coal-mining industry was vested in the National Coal Board. Alderman Ned Cowan is third from the right. The colliery closed in 1962.

Redheugh Gas Works during the Second World War. Gas and tar were important by-products of coal and during the war, women worked on quite heavy jobs like these which had previously been the preserve of men who were now serving in the armed forces. The lady on the right is Mrs Armstrong and next to her, by the word 'Works', is Mrs Isabella McMillan.

Making grindstones from rough blocks at Windy Nook Quarries in the early twentieth century. At one time, grindstones were exported all over the world from Gateshead but by this time the trade was in serious decline. Stone was subsequently quarried for building purposes but most quarries have since been filled in and built over.

Workers at Windy Nook Quarries, 1891. At this time, headgear was a significant indicator of status with the workers wearing cloth caps and only the supervisor wearing a trilby.

A damaged display board advertising John Abbot and Co., founded in 1825. Abbot's manufactured a huge range of products from locomotive engines, hydraulic presses, capstans, anchors and chains to water pipes, safety lamps and even nails and tacks. It was probably this lack of specialization which led to the company's demise in 1909.

Thomas Proctor and Son, engineers, c. 1901. It is significant that these firms tended to congregate along the riverside to gain ready access to transport by sea.

A beam engine manufactured by Hawks, Crawshay Ltd; the date is unknown. In its day Hawks was the biggest engineering firm in Gateshead and their greatest local monument is probably the High Level Bridge. The firm also built bridges elsewhere and diversified into ships' engines and the like. The company closed suddenly in 1889, possibly for similar reasons to Abbot's.

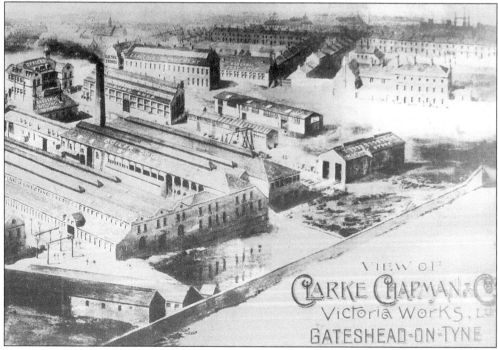

Clarke Chapman, founded 1862. This is the only large engineering firm to have survived to the present day. In the nineteenth century it manufactured winches, pumps, boilers and generators.

Clarke Chapman foremen's outing to Barnard Castle in 1895. Again, the headgear count here is interesting (see p. 20): there are six bowler hats (presumably a step up from trilbies), one trilby, one straw hat and two cloth caps. Possibly the last two had just been promoted.

Workers at Clarke Chapman before the First World War. In this case the headgear consists exclusively of caps.

Workers at Clarke Chapman in the First World War. What the occasion was is unknown but it is interesting that the two men in uniform are both lance-corporals. The man on the left-hand end of the front row also appears to be wearing a mixture of uniform and civilian clothes. Possibly it was a recruiting event.

The Velocycle, patented in 1887. This machine was designed by Edward Butler, an employee of Clarke Chapman. It included a forerunner of the modern carburettor but was never developed commercially.

Allhusen's works, c. 1910. Allhusen's was the largest of the chemical firms on Tyneside in the nineteenth century but was absorbed into the United Alkali Company which moved to Tees-side in the early years of the twentieth century.

Bleach packers in the chemical industry, c. 1910. The fumes in and around chemical works were extremely dangerous to health, and it was common practice for workers in the industry to wear several thicknesses of flannel over their faces while at work.

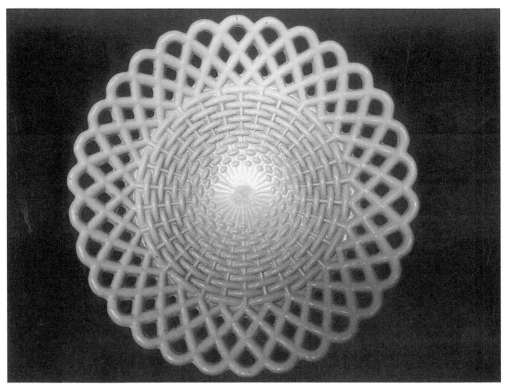

An example of the pressed or moulded glass which was made in imitation of cut glass by the two main glass manufacturers in Gateshead – George Davidson & Co. and Sowerby & Co.

A presentation to an employee for sixty years of service at George Davidson & Co.'s glass factory. The date is unknown, but those present are, from left to right, Messrs Carter, Hughes and Cobitt.

Last of the pipemakers, 1935. At one time Gateshead was a major centre for the manufacture of clay pipes with as many as ten pipemakers in the early nineteenth century. In 1898, one pipemaker, Francis Joseph Finn, even became mayor of the borough. The last of the pipemakers was George Stonehouse, whose shop, shown here, closed in 1935.

Tucker and Co., brewers. One industry which always had a steady clientele was brewing. Tucker and Co. occupied premises in the centre of the town for many years.

Team Valley Trading Estate under construction, 1936. This development was intended to relieve unemployment by providing attractive buildings and services for businesses coming to the town. This photograph shows the River Team canalized through the middle of the estate. (Compare the pictures on this page with those on p. 14.)

Team Valley Trading Estate under construction, 1936. This shows the 174-foot wide main road through the estate, now called Kingsway. At the time of its construction it was the widest road in England.

Two

The Victorian Riverside

From medieval times, most of the inhabitants of Gateshead not involved in farming, coal-mining or quarrying lived on the steep bank running down to the single bridge over the river.

In the early years of the nineteenth century, both industry and housing were concentrated in Bottle Bank and Bridge Street, which formed the main route up and down the bank, with adjoining alleyways, Bankwell Stairs (subsequently Lane) and Mirk Lane. The riverbank to the west was known as Rabbit Banks, and Pipewellgate and Hillgate were very narrow roads running parallel to the river in westerly and easterly directions respectively.

The houses in this area were situated cheek by jowl with industrial concerns, tended to be in very poor physical condition, were damp and dirty, and lacked the most basic amenities. Many of these buildings, particularly in Hillgate, were destroyed in the great fire and explosion of 1854. The rest survived until the 1930s when the council acquired the legal powers to clear the whole area.

A general view of the riverside area in 1925. At this stage some piecemeal demolition had already taken place but the very poor condition of the remaining buildings is quite apparent.

Another view of the same area in 1935. The Housing Act which came into effect in 1934 gave local authorities the power to deal with slum properties, and the council initiated a methodical programme of demolition in the riverside area which was largely completed by 1936.

Bottle Bank, *c.* 1905. A view up the bank from Bridge Street. The photograph was probably taken very early on a Sunday morning. Even so, the absence of even a single pedestrian is quite remarkable.

The view from the top of Bottle Bank, *c.* 1924. This would have been a more familiar view, with many pedestrians in evidence. Bottle Bank was so extremely steep that Church Street was built in 1790 as a very early 'bypass' for wheeled traffic, which left Bottle Bank as an almost completely traffic free area.

Half-way down the bank, again around 1924. This and the preceding views were about to change dramatically. The buildings on the east (right-hand) side of Bottle Bank were demolished in 1926, together with most of those in Bridge Street and Church Street, for the construction of access roads and piers for the new Tyne Bridge.

Bottle Bank in 1948. A sad end for an old medieval road.

A sketch of Pipewellgate in 1889. This probably conjures up the atmosphere of the area very well. Note the train crossing the High Level Bridge in the background.

Pipewellgate in the 1920s. This photograph suggests that little had changed since 1889.

Providence Place, Pipewellgate, in the early twentieth century. This is a good illustration of the poor conditions in which people were living.

Mortuary in Pipewellgate, 1935. There seems to have been little dignity even in death.

A house on Bankwell Stairs, c. 1886. The house is obviously nearing the end of its life but its interesting structure leads one to wonder about its history.

Bankwell Stairs in 1973. At this stage, Bankwell Stairs still survived in their original form, albeit against a background of the Tyne Bridge, a multi-storey office block and the modernized junction of Bottle Bank and Church Street.

An entry in Mirk Lane, *c.* 1886. These buildings dated from 1740.

Church Street, looking downhill, in 1924. With the exception of St Mary's church all these buildings were demolished in 1926 for the construction of the Tyne Bridge.

Church Street looking uphill, 1924. Notice the rather stylish gas lamp.

Another view of Church Street in 1924. The High Level Bridge is in the background. Despite the advent of the motor car at least one horse and cart team was still in business.

Houses in Church Walk, *c.* 1921.
The wall on the right surrounds
St Mary's churchyard. The houses
were demolished in 1933.

Tenements in Church Walk,
c. 1921. These were also demolished
in 1933. Church Walk had been
particularly badly hit in the cholera
outbreak of 1853 so their demolition
was long overdue.

Veitch's Buildings, Rabbit Banks Road, *c*. 1934. This building was particularly badly affected during the 1853 cholera outbreak but was not demolished until 1936.

The rear of two houses in Rabbit Banks Road, *c*. 1934. They were also demolished in 1936.

Houses in Bowl Alley, c. 1934. Another illustration of the poor-quality housing in which people were forced to live.

The Plough Yard, c. 1927: yet more poor-quality housing. This yard led to what were known as 'Crutchy Tom's Stairs', presumably named after a local character.

Three

The Town Centre

The continued growth of industry and population created a demand for more and better-quality housing, and from about 1820 onwards, people who could afford it began to move away from the riverside area. Housing began to spread southward from the top of the bank and, by about 1850, the northern ends of High Street and West Street (formerly Back Lane) were largely built up as far south as Jackson Chare (now Street).

Civic awareness was also growing. The town acquired its first MP in 1832, a town council and mayor in 1835 and, in due course, a Town Hall. From the beginning, however, the council suffered from a lack of resources due to the low rateable value of much of the property in the town. In addition, unlike many other local authorities, Gateshead left the operation of profitable public services like street lighting and water supply in the hands of private owners. The police and fire services were a major interest, but education did not become a council responsibility until 1902, and public housing was very much a twentieth-century development.

Bolivar Place, off High Street, built in 1825. This short road of stone-built houses dated from the early stages of the shift away from the riverside. The photograph was taken in 1936 and the houses were demolished in the following year.

Burn Street, built in 1867. To modern eyes, accustomed to rapid change, it is noteworthy that these houses, in the Chandless area, were almost identical in design to the Bolivar Place houses built forty years earlier apart from the use of brick instead of stone. They were demolished in 1958.

Nun's Lane, off High Street, built before 1838. More stone-built houses but in this case they are of mixed design. Like Bolivar Place, these houses were demolished in 1937.

Nelson Street, between High Street and West Street. These brick-built houses were demolished in 1939.

The north end of the High Street, *c.* 1902. High Street was almost entirely a commercial thoroughfare and subject to constant change.

High Street, north end, *c.* 1900. An affluent-looking family hurries along, possibly to catch a tram. Note the steam-driven tram in the background.

The buildings seen here on the right-hand side of the north end of the High Street were largely demolished during the construction of the Tyne Bridge in 1925. Snowball's began as a drapers in 1850 but grew into a large department store. It continued in business despite the loss of its frontage during the Tyne Bridge construction but finally closed down during the Second World War.

Old High Street shops, 1911. These old shops reflect some of Gateshead's more distant past. From left to right, J. Gaddes made footwear, R. Preston was a brush manufacturer, F. Collier a clay pipe manufacturer, Scott and Crow were horse shoers, farriers and general smiths, and T.A. Moffit was an ironmonger.

Lamb's Buildings, *c.* 1881. This small group of shops stood at the junction of High Street and Jackson Chare (later Street) on what was known as Busyburn Quay. They represented a relic of Gateshead's rural past, comprising a hay and straw dealer, clog makers and a joiner. As the 'modern' High Street expanded, they were demolished in 1896 and replaced initially by the Metropole Theatre.

A little further south along the High Street, *c.* 1918. The ornate building on the left is the Metropole Hotel (originally built as the Metropole Theatre in 1896).

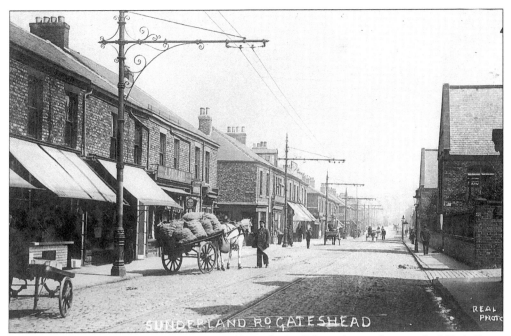

Sunderland Road, *c.* 1910. Sunderland Road branched off from the southern end of High Street and its western end developed as a shopping area to cater for the housing built to the east of the town centre.

Robbers' Corner, 1896. This attractive cottage was at one time the lodge at the entrance to the Park estate and stood at the junction of Sunderland Road and John Street. It was demolished around the turn of the twentieth century. The origin of its name is unknown.

The end of the Sunderland Road, 1886. This timber building had a chequered history. It apparently started life as a railway building at either Newcastle Central station or Redheugh and was re-erected here before the middle of the nineteenth century. It was demolished in 1904 and a theatre/cinema (called successively the Alhambra, King's, Empire and Essoldo) erected on the site (see p. 107).

West Street, c. 1900. This view is looking north from the junction with Jackson Street (to the right) and Walker Terrace (to the left) with the Savings Bank on the corner.

West Street, c. 1920, from almost the same position as the picture at the bottom of the previous page. Apart from the changes in fashion and the replacement of horses and carts by motor vehicles, the scene has changed little during the twenty years separating the two photographs.

A fire at Shephard's Ltd, 5 January 1946. Shephard's was another large department store, in West Street, which also had a number of branch shops in the area. The main store was destroyed by fire in 1946 and was rebuilt and re-opened in 1951. The firm later closed down and the site is now a car park.

49

Gateshead's first Town Hall in Oakwellgate, used from 1836 to 1844. After the first few meetings, which took place in temporary accommodation, the council rented this property in 1836 and occupied it until 1844 when they purchased another building near the railway station. This second Town Hall was used until 1867 when it had to be demolished because of railway extensions.

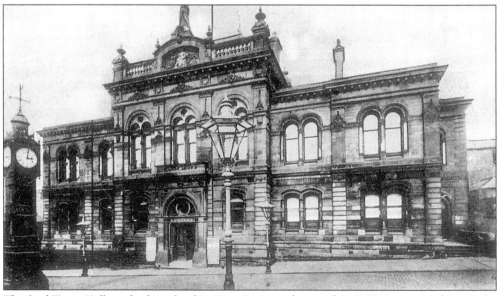

The final Town Hall was built on land in West Street and opened in 1870. It remained in use for over a century until it was replaced by the present Civic Centre

A celebration outside the Town Hall, c. 1900. The nature of the celebration is not known but may well have been the relief of Mafeking during the Boer War, which was the subject of much jubilation at the time.

William Swinburne, solicitor and Town Clerk of Gateshead from 1893 to 1929. Before William's appointment, his father, Joseph William, had served as Town Clerk from 1856 to 1893, so that father and son served for a combined total of seventy-three years. Indeed, the first ever council meeting in 1835 had been held in the offices of his grandfather, Thomas, who narrowly missed appointment as the first Town Clerk, which could have resulted in a continuous family service of ninety-four years. The family firm is still prominent in the Gateshead business world.

Swinburne Street in the 1920s. The contribution of the Swinburne family to Gateshead is acknowledged in the name of this street which runs along the north side of the Town Hall and at one time housed several council departments including the library.

Gateshead Police Band, 1872. From left to right, back row: Miles Swinburne, George Lennox, -?-, Isaac Moffit, ? Wood, James Clark, Ferguson Moore. Middle row: James Mackey, Dixon Brown, Adam Lunam, George Hogg, -?-, -?-, Alexander Murray, ? Turnbull. Front row: John Amos (Bandmaster), Peter Lundgren, William Todd, James Trotter, George Trotter, -?-, Edward Reed (Band Sergeant). In the foreground: William Brown (drummer) and an unidentified drummer boy.

Gateshead Borough Police/Fire Specials, 1918. The force was marching along Walker Terrace. The occasion is not known.

Gateshead Borough police, 1925. It is worth noting the presence of members of the fire service in this and the previous photograph. Until the Second World War, the fire service was regarded as an integral part of the police service.

Gateshead fire service, *c.* 1895. Gateshead firemen grouped round a recently acquired steam fire engine. The berets and moustaches give the service a very Gallic flavour at this point in its history.

Horse-drawn fire engines in the 1900s. These photographs were taken outside the Town Hall presumably on some formal occasion. The berets have now been replaced with traditional firemen's helmets.

Four

Western Gateshead

The great expansion of housing away from the old town centre took place following the break-up of the great estates of the landed gentry who owned most of the western areas of the borough before the 1860s.

Some growth had already begun with the enclosure of the town fields in Bensham and Windmill Hills in 1814, but the sale of the large Gateshead Park (the remains of the Bishop of Durham's hunting park), the Askew family's Redheugh estate, the Shipcote and Saltwellside estates, together with smaller estates like Field House and Derwent Crook, allowed the town to expand very rapidly. By the end of the nineteenth century, virtually the whole of the western area of the borough as far as the River Team had been built up.

Many large private houses were also built for local industrialists around this time, especially along the southern parts of Durham Road, but sadly these ceased to be economically viable in the twentieth century and have mostly been demolished.

Walker Terrace, *c.* 1900. Bensham Road was the main route to the west (it had originally been a toll road) and initially provided a natural core around which development took place. This view was from West Street along Walker Terrace, which formed the eastern end of Bensham Road. St Joseph's Roman Catholic church is on the left and the Savings Bank on the right (see also p. 49).

Bensham Road, *c.* 1900. This view is from the other end of Walker Terrace, looking back towards West Street.

Coatsworth Road, *c.* 1910. This street, which runs southwards off Bensham Road, was built in the 1860s and named (but mis-spelled) after William Cotesworth, the former lord of the manor and a prominent local businessman.

Coatsworth Road, *c.* 1910. With the development of the big housing estates to the west of the town centre, Coatsworth Road became, and remains today, a busy local shopping street.

Coatsworth Road, *c.* 1910. A quiet moment in a busy street. The relative absence of traffic, in this and the two previous photographs, is probably the most striking difference between these old pictures and the present day.

Hall Terrace in 1944. Hall Terrace ran off Coatsworth Road. It was built in the 1850s and was demolished in 1971.

Interior of 8 Hall Terrace, early 1900s. This suggests a fairly affluent style of living which was probably enjoyed by most of the residents of Hall Terrace at that time.

Three members of the Ord family who occupied 8 Hall Terrace in the early twentieth century. Here again the quality of dress suggests a comfortable style of living.

St Cuthbert's church, Bensham, c. 1900. At this point, Bensham Road continues downhill to the left heading towards the ancient High Team Bridge over the River Team, and Derwentwater Road forks off to the right en route to the Low Team Bridge. (Nowadays the sharp right hand turn leads to the Redheugh Bridge over the Tyne.) This junction is now a very busy intersection controlled by traffic lights.

Bensham Avenue, c. 1900. This road runs off the south side of Bensham Road.

Bensham Road at its junction with James Street. These houses and those shown in the following three photographs were built in 1860 but were all demolished as part of a general clearance of old housing in 1971.

Bensham Road post office, photographed in 1979.

Property in Redheugh Road, built 1878.

Shops in Redheugh Road, built 1878.

Papermill Square, *c.* 1915. This stood on the site of Eslington Court and took its name from the adjoining paper mill. Mary Atkinson, on the left, was a seamstress with Snowball's, the Gateshead department store. The other lady, probably her daughter, was Isobella Hilda Atkinson.

Lobley Hill, *c.* 1910. This view is from Lobley Hill looking eastward over the Team Valley towards Gateshead. Lobley Hill itself, which was outside Gateshead at that time, is now a large housing estate and the Team Valley is occupied by the giant trading estate which bears its name.

OLD SALTWELL HALL, GATESHEAD

Saltwell Hall was built in the late sixteenth century, and altered in the eighteenth century. Rapid development meant that Gateshead lost many fine buildings whose owners could no longer afford to maintain them. Saltwell Hall was of great historic interest as the centre of the Saltwellside estate from which Saltwell Park, Saltwell Cemetery and part of the Team Valley Trading Estate were created. The hall itself was used as an isolation hospital until it was finally demolished in 1936.

Ferndene, c. 1910. Ferdene was built in the early 1850s by R.S. Newall, the rope manufacturer, and demolished in the 1920s. The interest here lies not in the house, but in the private observatory which Newall built in the grounds, in which he installed what was, at the time, the largest telescope in the world.

Five

Gateshead Fell

Prior to the nineteenth century, Gateshead Fell was essentially wild moorland covered with the remains of pit-working and quarrying, and over which the borough-holders and freemen had pasture rights. Its few inhabitants lived in scattered groups of cottages, many of which were built of turf – hence Sodhouse Bank. This began to change following an Enclosure Act obtained in 1809 when the hamlets began to develop into villages with new roads and houses and other institutions to match.

Low Fell emerged as a village in its own right early on and became a fashionable place to live, with an active social life. High Fell, on the other hand, could not have presented more of a contrast, because its population comprised mainly pitmen and quarrymen and their families, and it became a centre for radical politics. Other villages and hamlets, like Sheriff Hill (so called because it was the place at which the mayor of Newcastle met the Assize judges on their way from Durham), Carr Hill, Wrekenton, Blue Quarries and Deckham, followed equally varied patterns of development but were all gradually absorbed into the growing Gateshead conurbation.

Gateshead Fell from the west, c. 1935. This is a general view of the Fell from the western side of Team Valley.

Sodhouse Bank, Sheriff Hill, Gateshead.

Sodhouse Bank (now re-named Sheriff's Highway), Sheriff Hill, c. 1900. Sodhouse Bank was part of the old turnpike road, now known as the Old Durham Road, which ran from the old Tyne Bridge, up Bottle Bank and the High Street, over Gateshead Fell, and down the Long Bank to Birtley and on to Durham.

Durham Road, *c.* 1904. The Old Durham Road involved climbing steep banks over the Fell and in 1827 it was replaced as the main north/south route by the present Durham Road through Low Fell, which was much flatter, as shown here.

Durham Road, early 1900s. This section of the road, just south of Belle Vue Bank, was designed to segregate different sorts of traffic by means of a narrow road and wide footpath on the western side, separate from the main carriageway.

The New Cannon Inn, Durham Road. The proprietor of the Cannon Inn in Sheriff Hill, realising that the re-routing of the main road through Low Fell would affect his trade, built the New Cannon Inn at the junction of Durham Road and Beaconsfield Road. This rapidly became the centre of the social life in Low Fell.

The Three Tuns, Sodhouse Bank, *c.* 1910. Unlike the Cannon, the Three Tuns remained in Sheriff Hill and became a focal point for the High Fell community. In the 1830s, in particular, it served as a centre for reform meetings, benefit societies and other radical causes.

Durham Road in winter, 1886. The snowstorm at the beginning of March 1886 lasted for forty hours and there were further falls a fortnight later while clearing up was still in progress. Presumably the horse and cart were engaged in snow clearance. They certainly seem to have attracted the interest of a lot of children on both sides of the road.

Durham Road, near Lowrey's Lane, c. 1900. Note the steam tram: these replaced the horse-drawn trams in the interim period before the introduction of electric traction.

Cottages on Belle Vue Bank, off Durham Road, c. 1886. Although these thatched cottages appear to be derelict, they were in fact occupied at the time. The house in the background is Park View South.

Belle Vue Bank, Low Fell, showing houses built in the 1830s. This photograph was taken in the same bad winter as that shown on the previous page.

Houses in Belle Vue Bank, Low Fell, built in the 1830s. This quite small building was nevertheless occupied as two separate houses.

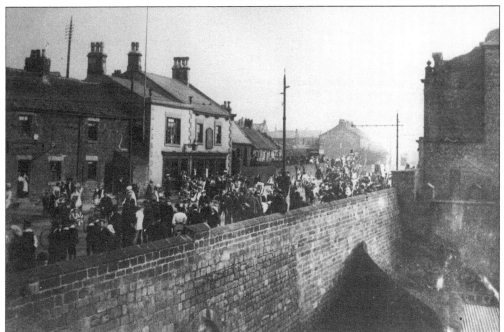

Durham Road, near Engine Lane, c. 1903. The light-coloured building in the centre is the Gateshead Arms. The gable end of Low Fell Co-op is on the right, Carter's Well (see p. 16) is at the foot of the wall in the foreground. Some sort of children's street parade seems to be in progress.

Another view of the same stretch of road as in the previous photograph but looking north with the Co-op on the left and the Gateshead Arms on the right.

Earl's Drive, Low Fell, *c.* 1900. This scene has changed enormously over the past century. Mr Minto, the general cartman, would now, no doubt, describe himself as a haulage contractor and would have difficulty in both buying coal and finding customers for it.

Chowdene Bank, Low Fell, *c.* 1900. Another rural scene quite different from the view today.

The tram terminus in Durham Road. Kells Lane is on the right.

Kells Lane, c. 1921. The person who sent this postcard asked 'Do you know where this is, Aunty?' It is actually a view looking up Kells Lane (at one time known as Lamesley Road) from its junction with Durham Road, as shown in the previous photograph, towards the Old Durham Road.

Orchard Cottage Dairy Farm, Kells Lane. This is another rural scene which survived until the Second World War.

Derwent Gardens, Low Fell, c. 1900. Some short distance to the east of Kells Lane, Derwent Gardens presents a street layout for a simpler lifestyle without cars and with space for children to play.

Beaconsfield Road, Low Fell, 1920s. This view looks down Beaconsfield Road (at one time Low Fell Road) from its junction with Kells Lane towards Durham Road.

Blue Quarries Road, 1938. These houses were photographed shortly before their demolition in the same year. The attractive outside appearance of old stone-built houses often concealed sub-standard conditions within.

Broadway, Sheriff Hill, c. 1920. By contrast with the previous photograph, these houses look long overdue for the demolition which has since overtaken them.

Six

Transport

In the past, few people travelled great distances away from their homes. As the population grew, however, people began travelling longer distances to work and for other purposes. This required better means of transport.

In Gateshead, hackney carriage services were introduced in 1827 but were very expensive, and horse omnibus services started in 1860. A tramway system was developed from 1883 but horses could not cope with the steep gradients and steam trams had to be used until 1901 when they were replaced by electric traction. Tram services were converted to bus services in 1950; the last tram ran in 1951 and by 1953 all the track and overhead wires had gone.

Gateshead was a railway town for many years. The major east/west line was officially opened in 1838 and the north/south line in 1844, but the system was much enlarged in subsequent years. The Greenesfield locomotive works and sheds were built in 1852 and the sheds at Park Lane in 1873. By the turn of the century the North Eastern Railway was the largest employer in Gateshead. The Greenesfield works closed in 1932 but most other closures – of the Park Lane sheds and several local railway stations – took place as traffic diminished after the Second World War.

Recreation of a Venture coach, 1939. This working replica of an early horse omnibus ran between Shotley and Edmundbyers between 1923 and 1939.

Horse bus, c. 1905. These horse buses ran across the High Level Bridge between Gateshead and Newcastle between 1883 and 1931 and were very well patronized. One good reason was that there was a pedestrian toll of a halfpenny to cross the bridge and, as the bus fare was exactly the same, the passengers were in effect getting the ride for nothing.

A steam tram in the High Street, *c.* 1890. Both Nestlé's Milk and Waddington's Pianos were well advertised.

A steam tram in Durham Road, *c.* 1890. This is a different view of the tram showing the access to the upper deck. Lipton's teas and Bryant and May's matches are two other names still familiar to us.

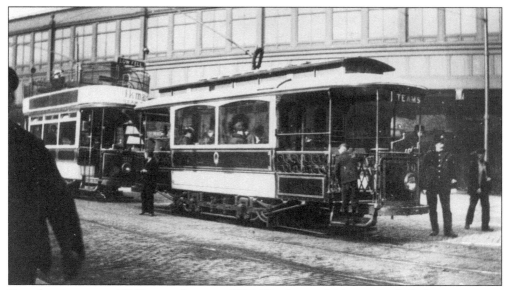

Two electric trams at Wellington Street, c. 1920. The front vehicle is a single-decker en route to the Teams. The rear vehicle is a double-decker heading for Low Fell but the upper deck is open to the elements.

Electric tram, 1912. This was an experimental pay-as-you-enter scheme as the instructions to 'Pay as you enter' and 'Have one penny ready' indicate. There were even separate sides of the platform for entry and exit to speed up access. Despite this, the scheme was not a success and caused considerable congestion.

The route to Dunston was the last tram route to close on 4 August 1951.

Clippies, c. 1916. Women took over tram conductors' jobs during the First World War – a significant step forward for women in their progress towards equal rights.

On 5 February 1916, a runaway tram overturned on Bensham Bank killing four people. This was possibly a consequence of the deterioration of the permanent way under wartime conditions.

A tram negotiates the curve in the track on Bensham Bank (at which the accident happened) shortly before final closure of the route in 1950.

An early motor bus, *c.* 1913. This early double-decker has solid rubber tyres and an open upper deck. At this stage, buses were still regarded as a two-person job. The driver is physically separated from the passengers and the conductor is collecting a fare on the upper deck.

A Leyland bus, *c.* 1920. This is a single-decker and the driver has been given more protection from the elements by incorporating the driver's seat into the passenger compartment (although there may still be a screen behind him) but the access is still from the rear, suggesting that a conductor was still required.

Daimler bus, c. 1923. On this single-decker the entrance has been moved to the front which suggests that the possibility of combining the jobs of driver and conductor had at least been considered.

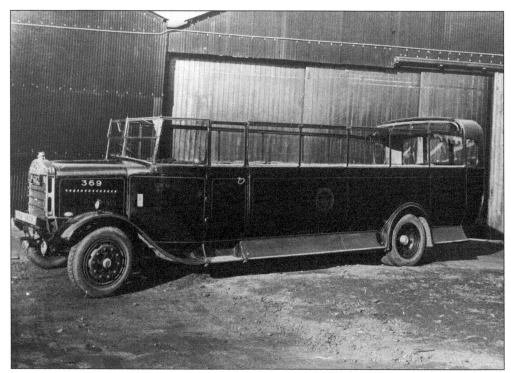

A charabanc, c. 1928. This is described as an 'all-weather' charabanc, which is presumably a reference to the retractable soft top.

Brandling station, built 1839. This station is actually in Felling, which only became part of Gateshead in 1974, but is included as a reminder of the Brandling Junction Railway which provided the original east/west railway line through Gateshead.

The *Aerolite*, built in 1851, was an example of the large number of locomotives built in the Greenesfield Works over the years. It is now in the National Railway Museum in York.

Locomotive No. 663, built in 1887. This was also built at Greenesfield but was not so lucky as *Aerolite*. While the engine was hauling a train from Liverpool on 19 August 1889, it ran too fast down Seaton Bank and was derailed on the curve at Ryhope. The rest of the train was also derailed and 101 passengers were injured.

An interesting experiment was this 'rail bus', a Leyland motor bus converted to run on rails in 1922. It was displayed at a railway cavalcade to celebrate the centenary of the Stockton and Darlington Railway in 1925.

The LNER Stores Department annual outing in 1910. On this occasion, the outing was to Jesmond Dene.

The LNER Stores Department staff at Gateshead West station in 1920. Some of the faces were also present in 1910 but others of the 1910 group had probably been casualties of the First World War.

Low Fell station, which stood at the foot of Station Road in Low Fell, closed on 7 April 1952. This photograph was taken in 1910.

Bensham station, which stood at the end of Elysium Lane, closed on 5 April 1954.

Seven

Bridges

Despite the increasing populations of the two boroughs, Gateshead and Newcastle remained linked by a single bridge at river level until the middle of the nineteenth century. The original bridge was Roman and, with repairs, lasted until 1248 when it was destroyed by fire. The next bridge, on the same site, lasted from 1250 until it was destroyed by flood in 1771. A replacement bridge was finally opened in 1781 but the need to allow ocean-going vessels to pass further upstream led to its demolition and the construction of the present Swing Bridge in 1876, at the time the largest swing bridge in the world.

Improvements to cross-river traffic finally came about because of the expansion of the railways which required a cross-river link at bank-top level. The solution was to build the High Level (road and rail) Bridge which was opened by Queen Victoria in 1849. Over the next seventy years, three further bridges were opened to deal with the increasing road and rail traffic – the Redheugh Bridge (road) in 1871 (but extensively re-built between 1897 and 1901), the King Edward Bridge (rail) in 1906 and the Tyne Bridge (road) in 1928 – thereby making up the famous 'Five Bridges'. Later in the twentieth century, a sixth bridge was added to carry the Metro railway and the Redheugh Bridge was demolished and replaced.

The old Tyne Bridge, opened 1781. In addition to preventing the passage upstream of any large vessel, this bridge had become structurally unsound due to undermining by dredging of the river; it was replaced by the Swing Bridge in 1876.

High Level Bridge, opened 1849. This photograph, of Newcastle and the High Level Bridge, was taken from Rabbit Banks in 1887. The bridge is a 'double-decker' with trains on top and a roadway below. Both George and Robert Stephenson were involved in its construction.

A tram on the High Level Bridge, *c.* 1923. There was a toll of a halfpenny on both pedestrians and vehicles using the bridge until 1937.

The Gateshead entrance to the High Level Bridge, *c.* 1923. Trams are leaving the road level and rail access to the upper level is on the right.

The Swing Bridge, opened in 1876. This photograph was taken in 1900 with the High Level Bridge behind. Because it was toll-free it was always well-used despite the steep banks which had to be negotiated on either side of the river.

The original Redheugh Bridge, built between 1868 and 1871. This photograph was taken in 1895 before the bridge was extensively rebuilt. Like the High Level Bridge, users had to pay a toll.

The original Redheugh Bridge after rebuilding between 1897 and 1901.

Old Redheugh Bridge being dismantled in 1984. The new Redheugh Bridge, which was opened by Princess Diana, is visible behind.

The King Edward Bridge under construction, c. 1905. At this stage it was generally referred to as the 'New High Level Bridge'. It acquired its official title from its opening by King Edward VII.

King Edward Bridge in 1964.

The Tyne Bridge approaches, between 1924 and 1926. Preparatory work for the new Tyne Bridge necessitated extensive demolition in Bridge Street, Church Street and Bottle Bank. This was very much a mixed blessing. A great deal of slum property was cleared away but at the same time many people were made homeless and some good houses were also destroyed.

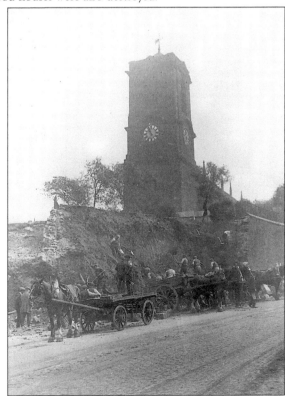

Even St Mary's churchyard was caught up in the demolition process leading to the construction of the Tyne Bridge in the mid-twenties.

The Tyne Bridge under construction, 16 December 1927. This view eastwards from the High Level Bridge shows the steelwork beginning to reach out from both sides of the river. The Swing Bridge is in the foreground.

Tyne Bridge construction, 17 February 1928. This view looks westwards and shows the arch almost complete. The High Level and Swing Bridges are in the background.

The completed Tyne Bridge, 1928. This is the view from the Gateshead side, again with the High Level and Swing Bridges in the background.

The official opening of the Tyne Bridge by King George V, 10 October 1928. Since then it has become a universally recognized symbol of Tyneside.

The last toll, 10 May 1937. The opening of the toll-free Tyne Bridge led eventually to the abolition of tolls on the High Level and Redheugh Bridges (the Swing Bridge had always been toll-free). The photograph shows the Lord Mayor of Newcastle paying the last toll at the Newcastle end of the High Level Bridge.

After being famous for its 'Five Bridges', the Tyne acquired a sixth bridge in 1977 when the Metro system was built. This shows the Queen Elizabeth Bridge under construction.

Eight

Leisure

Until the later years of the nineteenth century, leisure was an activity largely restricted to the wealthy classes. Working hours were long and pay was low, and in consequence, the time and money available for leisure were very limited. In addition, the difficulties involved in getting about before the development of public transport systems meant that any leisure pursuits which did exist tended to be fairly local in nature. In consequence, local pubs became the focus of community activity in many areas, evolving in some cases into 'music halls' or sponsoring sporting or other activities, as landlords competed for customers.

The first great spectator sports in the mid-nineteenth century were horse-racing and competitive rowing; association football only became really popular towards the end of the century. Quieter outdoor activities were associated with the new public parks, where trees and flowers could be enjoyed, and games like cricket, tennis and bowls could be played. Theatres and music halls were the main sources of indoor entertainment until the cinema came along, to be overtaken in turn by today's radio, television and video.

The Long Walk, Saltwell Park, c. 1910. Saltwell Park was created by Gateshead Council on what had been part of the old Saltwellside estate and opened in 1876. In addition to attractive landscaped areas like the Long Walk, it included a lake, bowls and tennis facilities, and a maze.

Saltwell Towers, c. 1910. The building now known as Saltwell Towers was originally built as a private residence in the mid-nineteenth century, but by the 1920s it was unoccupied and derelict. The council used it as a museum from 1932 until 1969 when dry rot forced its closure. It is interesting that the Shipley Art Gallery was created from a bequest from one of the former occupants of the Towers, J.A.D. Shipley, who died in 1909.

An example of the public house as a centre of social life: an excursion from the Alma public house in 1929. There is no indication of the nature of the trip but it is clearly a popular function – indeed, it looks as though half the (all male) passengers will have to walk unless there is another conveyance round the corner. The Alma stood at the corner of Park Lane and Hopper Street.

A street trip from Allhusen Terrace, c. 1923. It was not, of course, necessary to base every trip on a public house. This one is street-based and appears to include no men at all apart from the driver and his mate, and possibly the lad standing on the edge of the pavement.

Gateshead Football Club, 1913/14. This team used to play at Old Fold Park, where their record gate was 13,000, but the club went out of existence in 1919.

Redheugh Park, Teams, was created in 1930. South Shields FC officially changed its name to Gateshead FC in 1930 and Redheugh Park was laid out as its home ground. The ground also housed a greyhound track from 1936. The club and the ground closed down in 1972/73. By an odd coincidence, the present Gateshead FC was also acquired from South Shields.

NER Loco football team, in the early twentieth century. There were always, of course, a number of other football teams in the town. The NER, as the largest employer in the borough, supported its own football team. There are two different strips in this photograph, possibly because it was a pre-match photograph with one or two members of each team missing.

Bensham Villa AFC, Tyneside Amateur League Champions of 1916/17. The only man whose name is known is James Griffiths, better known as Candy Griff or Taffy, who is kneeling on the left-hand side of the photograph. A lifelong employee of Raine and Co. of Derwenthaugh, he was married in St Mary's church in 1915. The couple then moved to Dunston.

Low Fell Cricket Club, *c.* 1900.

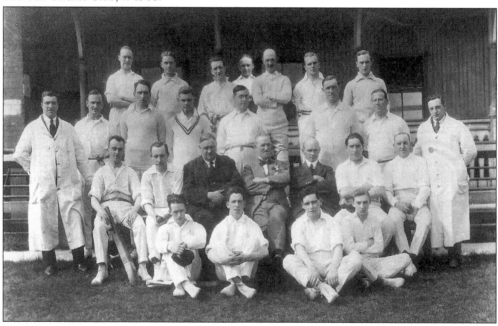

Tyneside Wednesday League, *c.* 1920. This shows the players in a match between married men and single men played at the North Durham ground in Prince Consort Road. There is no record of which were which, nor of which side won, but their names are, from left to right, back row: Bill Lauderdale, A. James, T. Fanhill, J. Stansfield, ? Bedford, N. Haswell, T. Smith. Third row: ? Clark, -?-, J. Tinker, G. Rigby, -?-, G. Cleavett, L. Rasen, ? Haworth. Second row (on chairs): Walter Sutton, N. Gleeholm, ? Patterson, Charlie Young, C. Rigby, C. Tinkler, E. Gleeholm. Front row (on ground): J. Chessman, C. Peacock, L. Peacock, Jim Smith.

Tynevale Amateur Cycling Club, 1895. Cycling was a very popular hobby in the late nineteenth century. The club captain, holding the bicycle at the front left of the picture, was George Brown, whose life reflected the rapid changes in society around that time. He started working life as a blacksmith, set up his own business and moved progressively from horses to bicycles, motor cycles and cars, helping to form the Gateshead Motor Club in 1922. He lived to the ripe old age of ninety-six.

Cycle races at the North Durham ground, *c.* 1910. By this time, cycle racing had been a feature of the sporting calendar for around thirty years.

Gateshead Civilian Rifle Club, *c.* 1900. Shooting was perhaps a more popular hobby in the past than today. It was obviously the age of the moustache, although two members (clearly the older generation) are wearing beards and four (equally clearly the younger generation) are clean-shaven.

Gateshead Tramways Rifle Club, 1931. The couple seated either side of the trophies are Mr Stagg, director, and his wife, presumably the donors of the Stagg Shield. The Morris Cup appears to be the same cup as that displayed by the Civilian Rifle Club thirty years earlier, but on this occasion only four moustaches, all very neatly trimmed, are visible.

Four well-known rowers, *c.* 1880. From left to right, back: B. Bagnall, J. Taylor. Front: T. Winship, J. Sadler.

Essoldo Cinema: opened 1905, demolished 1968. The history of the Essoldo is fairly typical of cinemas generally, moving by stages from being a theatre providing stage shows to being a cinema, under a series of different owners and with several changes of name. It was planned in 1904 as the Alhambra Theatre of Varieties, opened in 1905 as the King's Theatre, became the Empire Theatre in 1918 and finally the Essoldo in 1950. (The previous building on the site is shown on page 48.)

Palace Cinema: built 1909, closed 1960. By contrast with the Essoldo, the Palace was built primarily as a cinema but with a stage for variety turns between films, although these seem to have been phased out by about 1930.

Staff of the Shipcote Cinema, c. 1913. The Shipcote was built in 1911 at the junction of Durham Road and Dryden Road. At that time, it seated about 1200 people and had a resident orchestra, so that the need for a staff of twenty-seven is perhaps not surprising.

Nine

Churches and Schools

St Mary's was the only Anglican church in Gateshead until the early years of the nineteenth century when the growth in population necessitated a rapid expansion. Around the same time, the various strands of non-conformist thinking were already well-represented by a large number of chapels, although many of these were very small. The resurgence of Roman Catholicism was marked by the appointment of a parish priest in 1850 and the opening of St Joseph's church in High West Street in 1859. Many other faiths were represented in the town which nowadays also enjoys an international reputation as a centre for Jewish learning.

As in other parts of the country, the churches played a major role in early education provision, but there were also schools attached to factories, and 'private' schools which provided education of a variable, but generally low, quality. Modern universal education may be said to have begun in 1870 with the appointment of the first Gateshead School Board which began building schools to fill the gaps in existing provision, a policy carried on by its successor, Gateshead Education Committee, from 1920 onwards.

St Mary's church, *c.* 1910. In the past, the political role of the church was often as great as its spiritual role. In Gateshead, St Mary's church was the centre of all aspects of town life, and prior to the election of the first town council in 1835, many of the functions of a modern council were undertaken by the church's 'select vestry', a self-appointing body generally known as the 'four-and-twenty'.

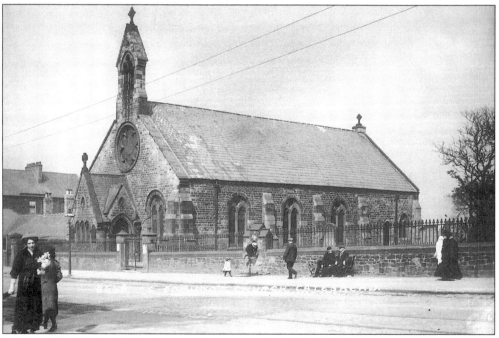

St Edmund's church, Old Durham Road, *c.* 1900. This church was originally the medieval chapel of King James' Hospital, rebuilt in 1810.

St John's church, Gateshead Fell, *c.* 1828. This church was built following the enclosure of Gateshead Fell and opened in 1825. The first Rector was William Hawks, a relative of George Hawks, the ironmaster who later became the first Mayor of Gateshead.

Holy Trinity church, *c.* 1893. The original building on the site dates from 1248 when it was St Edmund's Hospital. The ruins were given to the church by Cuthbert Ellison, a member of a prominent local family, rebuilt and enlarged by public subscription and opened as Holy Trinity in 1837.

St Cuthbert's church, Bensham, *c.* 1875. This church is another product of public generosity. The land was acquired at a nominal price from another well-known local family, the Askews, and the building was financed by public subscription with Cuthbert Ellison making a substantial donation.

Methodist Central Hall, High West Street, 1979. Originally built as a Wesleyan Chapel in 1860, the building was converted into the Methodist Central Hall in 1933.

St Joseph's church, High West Street, opened 1859. Like some of the Anglican churches mentioned on previous pages, St Joseph's was largely financed by public subscription, with working men paying one shilling per month. It remained the only Roman Catholic church in Gateshead until Our Lady and St Wilfred's was built in Sunderland Road in 1904.

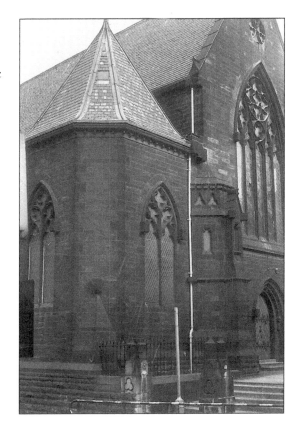

Papermill Square Mission, 1905. This is an example of one of the evangelical movements which were also active in the town around the turn of the twentieth century.

Amen Corner, c. 1900. The junction of High West Street and Durham Road acquired this name because of the presence of three churches – Baptist, Presbyterian and Methodist. The construction of the Gateshead Highway led to the complete re-modelling of the junction and the Swallow (formerly Five Bridges) Hotel now stands on the site of the Presbyterian church.

Children of Burn Street, 1906. When looking at Gateshead's schools of 100 years ago, it is important to remember the poverty which existed in many parts of the town. Only one of the children seen in this photograph is wearing shoes – a sight we would now associate with only the very poorest nations.

Grant Street School, built 1877. The photograph was taken in 1971 when the school was approaching its centenary.

Children at Grant Street School, 1889. The children in this and the next two groups appear to be better dressed than the children of Burn Street but they may, of course, come from better-off backgrounds or may be wearing their 'go-to-school' clothes, not available for street play.

Children at St Mary's Church of England School, *c.* 1890.

Children of High Street Wesleyan School, 1920/21. In this case, the names of most of the boys and two of the girls (the reason for the sex discrimination is not known) have been preserved as follows. From left to right, back row: The only named child is Carrie Atkinson, second from right. Third row: C. Ridley, W. Graham, R. Gray, R. Raeburn, G. Raine, D. Robson, -?-. Second row: the only named child is Alice Gamester, second from left. Front row: R. Hawdon, F. Ferry, W. Philips, W. Blair, R. Wilson, D. Wood, C. Finch.

Gateshead Grammar School, Durham Road, c. 1910. At this time, before comprehensive education, there were very few secondary school places available in the borough, this being the only grammar school. In consequence, only a tiny proportion of the population could expect to receive secondary school education.

Pupils at Gateshead Higher Grade School, Whitehall Road, 1889. It is perhaps a sign of the times that, although the pupils are female, both the teachers pictured are male.

Mechanics Institute, built 1848. The Institute was intended to provide voluntary post-school educational services, including lectures and a library service, before these facilities were provided by the council. By the turn of the century, despite its name, few working-class people were involved and its activities were largely social. The building was sold in 1907 and became a bank before its demolition in 1971.

Evacuation, 2 September 1939. Evacuation away from potential targets for bombing during the Second World War interrupted many children's education. In this photograph, outside Gateshead West station, the Mayor is seeing off a group of mothers and children.

Ten

People and Events

Like most places of any size, Gateshead's history contains many names of famous people. Some of these are people whose contributions to the arts and sciences have made them nationally, or even internationally, known and respected. Others have achieved recognition for their wealth and power, or for their services to the community. Yet others have been local 'personalities' or eccentrics. This section includes a few of these. Unfortunately, pictures of some of these people – William Cotesworth, for example – just do not seem to be available.

Events fall into similar categories. There are local events with national repercussions, local manifestations of national events, and local events which have just local significance. This section also records only a small selection of these. As with people, the events included have had to be determined by what photographs are available rather than by any more meaningful yardstick.

George Hawks, first Mayor of Gateshead, 1835. Hawks, head of the iron manufacturing firm of that name, had the distinction of being one of Gateshead's first councillors and aldermen, and its first Mayor. He served two further terms as Mayor in 1848 and 1849, when he bought a red robe and cocked hat for future Mayoral use.

Isaac Charles Johnson, Mayor in 1864. He also owned a Portland Cement Works in the town. Johnson subsequently lived to be 100 years old and is seen here reading a letter of congratulation from the king.

Thomas Bewick, wood engraver, 1753-1828. Bewick is probably best known for his illustrations of country life. Before coming to live in Gateshead, Bewick spent his childhood in Cherryburn which has now been turned into a museum dedicated to his work.

Bewick's house in West Street, undated. The site is now occupied by Gateshead Post Office.

Sir Joseph Swan, physicist and chemist, 1828-1914. His best-known invention was probably the electric lamp (before Edison), but he also developed artificial silk and made several inventions in the field of photography. The photograph was taken at Christmas 1910.

Underhill, Swan's house in Kells Lane, Low Fell, built around 1869.

Three Gateshead characters from the late nineteenth century. From left to right: Sawdust Jack, Coffee Johnny and Tommy on the Bridge. Tommy on the Bridge (Thomas Ferens, 1841-1907) was a blind man who spent most of his life begging in the middle of the old Tyne Bridge, and later on the Swing Bridge, in the belief that this position made him safe from both the Gateshead and Newcastle police forces.

Celebrations for the Diamond Jubilee of Queen Victoria in Saltwell Park, 22 June 1897. Over 12,000 children attended this celebration and each received a commemorative medal. Gateshead College now stands in the area beyond the trees where the houses then stood.

A welcome party in Newton Street, Bensham, 1902. The reason for the welcome is not known. It may have been to welcome a neighbour back from the Boer War which finished in that year.

Visit of King Edward VII, 1906. The king visited Gateshead in that year to open the King Edward Bridge.

This giant bonfire was created to celebrate the coronation of King George V on 22 June 1911.

The Durham Light Infantry are shown marching along Brighton Avenue before embarking for France to fight in the First World War, 1915.

Inter-Council bowls match in 1923. This match was against Newcastle Council in Saltwell Park. The mayor was Sir John Maccoy who was serving his eighth term of office in that year – the greatest number of terms ever served by a mayor of Gateshead. Nowadays, mayors are restricted to a single year.

Gateshead Carnival, 1927 – a reminder of simpler pleasures. Gateshead and District Burns Club won first prize for this tableau showing the Cotter's Saturday Night, with transport courtesy of Gateshead Co-operative Society.

King George V inspects the 9th Battalion Durham Light Infantry, 10 October, 1928. This event took place in Prince Consort Road on the occasion of the opening of the Tyne Bridge.

VE Day celebrations, Exeter Street, 14 May 1945. Many such street parties were held across the country to celebrate the end of the Second World War.

Acknowledgements

Many people have helped in the preparation of this book but I must say particular words of thanks to Eileen Carnaffin, of the Local Studies Section of Gateshead Libraries Service. Eileen has been a tower of strength, particularly when illness in my family put the whole project into suspense, and I cannot thank her enough for all her help.

Gateshead Libraries Service has also provided most of the photographs. Their photographic collection contains thousands of items and is a magnificent source of information about the history of the borough. I have also found several books about Gateshead's history written by Frank Manders, a former member of Gateshead Libraries staff, enormously helpful.

Other people who have helped me by offering me the loan of photographs, letters and other material (not all of which I have been able to take up, unfortunately) or by just talking to me about their memories, and whom I should like to thank, include Mr D. Allen, Mrs N. Banks, Mr E. Bone, Councillor L. Carr, Mr C. Gallimore, Mr Gibson, Mrs Gordon, Mr J. Henderson, Councillor M. Henry, Mrs E. Hetherington, Mr S. McCrae, Mrs M. Medd, Mr C. Swinburne, Mrs Watson.

To all the above people, and to anyone else I may have inadvertently omitted, I should like to express my gratitude.

Alan Brazendale